Sketches on THE LONG MARCH

Sketches on
THE LONG MARCH

by HUANG ZHEN

FOREIGN LANGUAGES PRESS

First Edition 2006

Home Page:
http://www.flp.com.cn
E-mail Addresses:
info@flp.com.cn
sales@flp.com.cn

ISBN 7-119-04514-8

Published by the Foreign Languages Press
24 Baiwanzhuang Road, Beijing100037, China
Distributed by China International Book Trading Corporation
35 Chegongzhuang Xilu, Beijing 100044, China
P. O. Box 399, Beijing, China

Printed in the People's Republic of China

Note on the New Edition

In 1982, the Foreign Languages Press published the English edition of *Sketches on the Long March,* which included 24 sketches drawn by General Huang Zhen as an authentic record of the Long March. Over the past two decades, the English edition has proved popular with readers both at home and abroad. This year marks the 70th anniversary of the victory of the Long March. To commemorate this great event and Red Army officers and men like General Huang, we are presenting a new edition of the album with revisions and a new design.

Besides recording the heroic undertaking of the Long March, the album is also a commemoration of the Long March spirit.

Foreign Languages Press
July 2006

Contents

Publisher's Note

The Chinese Workers' and Peasants' Red Army undertook the world-shaking 25,000-*li* (12,500-kilometre) Long March from 1934 to 1936. The 24 sketches by Huang Zhen collected in this album are a fragmentary but true record of the Long March. At the beginning of the War of Resistance Against Japanese Aggression (1937-1945), the sketches were collected in book form and published in Shanghai. In 1958, nine years after the founding of New China, the People's Fine Arts Publishing House, Beijing, republished them using the Shanghai edition as the master copy. Since then, the sketches have been reprinted twice, and we are publishing this book on the basis of the 1962 edition, *Sketches on the Long March*, printed by the People's Fine Arts Publishing House with a preface by Xiao Hua and a history by A Ying, editor of the original Shanghai publication.

The artist himself has provided captions for each picture. A cadre at the time of the Long March, Huang Zhen went on to become a general before assuming diplomatic and then ministerial positions.

Preface

by Xiao Hua[1]

This *Sketches on the Long March* was originally entitled *Sketches on the Journey to the West.* When its second edition was prepared in 1958, it was not known who the artist was. He was thought to be a comrade doing publicity work in the Fifth Army Corps of the Red Army. Now we are delighted to learn that the painter is Comrade Huang Zhen.

As a participant in the Long March, I was asked to write a preface for the 1962 edition of *Sketches on the Long March* by Comrade Huang Zhen published by the People's Fine Arts Publishing House to

---

[1] Xiao Hua (1916-1985) was director of the General Political Department of the People's Liberation Army and a member of the Standing Committe of the Central Military Commission.

commemorate the twentieth anniversary of the publication of "Talks at the Yan'an Forum on Literature and Art" by Comrade Mao Zedong. I am delighted to do so.

Thumbing through this book, I can hardly hold back my heartfelt emotions. These drawings and paintings revive my memory of things more than twenty years ago. Many unforgettable scenes again appear before my eyes: the all-year-round snow-capped Jiajin Mountains; the endless grasslands; the turbulent Dadu River; the bonfires in the deep mountains and forests; the wind and sandstorms on the northwest plateau;... Many comrades rest forever in the frozen snow. And many comrades left the road of the Long March stained with their blood. When they fell down, they all cherished deep in their hearts the firm belief: The Chinese people will surely stand up and get rid of the fetters of thousands of years and build a new state of their own.

Under the leadership of the Communist Party of China headed by Comrade Mao Zedong, the Workers' and Peasants' Red Army, after experiencing untold hardships and surmounting innumerable and incredible difficulties, concluded successfully the Long March covering a distance of 25,000 *li*, thus accomplishing a miracle unique in history.

Today, the ideal of those comrades who laid down their lives during the Long March has come true. The Chinese people under the leadership of the Communist Party of China are pioneering a cause unprecedented in history. Socialist construction is marching forward in big and stable strides. The heroism displayed by the Chinese Workers' and Peasants' Red Army during the Long March will always inspire our people to brave all difficulties and hardships, confront dangers and obstacles and work hard and diligently to create a still better life. In this book, the artist writes: "High as the snow mountain is, still higher is the iron will of this iron Red Army!" These proud words from the bottom of the Red Army fighters' hearts will remain loud and inspiring forever like a clarion call. These 24 sketches are a fragmentary record of the great Long March. They supply important data of revolutionary history and are precious works of art.

With hundreds of thousands of fighters, Huang Zhen travelled thousands of miles in this militant army, recording these touching scenes of history. These sketches are indeed soul-stirring. The artist depicted in bold relief the revolutionary optimism of the Red Army fighters. He also recorded scenes of those areas where the national minorities lived and the sufferings of the poor people. Even today there are not many works of art like these. We sincerely hope that comrades will follow this example to produce more works that give more vigorous expression to the new life in our great socialist age.

April 1962

Comrade Lin Boqu (1885-1960), a Chinese proletarian revolutionary, in his early days joined the Revolutionary League to help lead the Revolution of 1911. In the 1920s, he played an important role in helping Sun Yat-sen formulate his Three Principles — unite with the Soviet Union, unite with the Chinese Communist Party and support peasants and workers — and in reorganizing the Kuomintang. In 1927, he took part in the Nanchang Uprising and after that served as Minister of Finance of the Central Democratic Government in Jiangxi.

Like veterans Xu Teli,[1] Dong Biwu[2] and Xie Juezai,[3] Comrade Lin Boqu was a grey-haired man of over 50 during the Long March. Near-sighted, he always wore a pair of thick glasses and often carried a barn lantern in his left hand and held a stick in his right. The participation of these old men in the Long March gave great inspiration to both commanders and fighters of the Red Army.

The world-shaking Long March also found the participation of celebrated leaders, including Mao Zedong, Zhou Enlai, Liu Shaoqi and Zhu De. They were not only commanders directing the Red Army but also ordinary people who fought and lived side by side with thousands of other commanders and fighters, really living in the hearts of all the Red Army soldiers. They shared the joys and sorrows of their men, giving them boundless confidence and strength. Together with the Red Army soldiers, they entered the Miao villages, slept by the fire in the Yao people's kitchens and put up for the night in Yi huts and Tibetan "cow dung houses." They climbed the snow-covered Jiajin Mountains, crossed untrodden grasslands, led soldiers into battles, braved violent storms to hold meetings in the remote mountains and rode rafts to cross the turbulent rivers. Side by side with the soldiers, they conquered the high peaks of Mount Liupan to arrive finally at the border of the Shaanxi-Gansu Revolutionary Base Area.

---

[1] Xu Teli (1877-1968) was a proletarian revolutionary and educationist. He was a member of the Eighth Central Committee of the Chinese Communist Party before his death.

[2] Dong Biwu (1885-1975) was a founder of the Chinese Communist Party. After the founding of new China in 1949, he held a number of posts such as Vice-Chairman and Acting Chairman of the People's Republic of China as well as Vice-Chairman of the Standing Committee of the National People's Congress.

[3] Xie Juezai (1883-1971) was the President of the Supreme People's Court of China before his death.

夜行軍中的老英雄

1 *Comrade Lin Boqu – an Old Hero on a Night March*

On October 16, 1934, the First Front Army of the Chinese Workers' and Peasants' Red Army left the Central Revolutionary Base Area in south Jiangxi and Fujian provinces to start the world-renowned Long March. After thirty-eight days of fierce fighting, the troops broke through the enemy's encirclement by crushing three so-called strategic blockade lines, crossed the Xiaoshui River in Daozhou in Hunan and headed for the Xiangjiang River. The victory of the Red Army startled the Kuomintang reactionaries. Chiang Kai-shek hurriedly dispatched 400,000 troops, divided into three routes, to pursue and intercept the Red Army. Pouring in from all directions, they merged to form a fourth-line of defence on the east bank of the Xiangjiang, between the Xiangjiang and Xiaoshui rivers, in an attempt to trap and eliminate the Red Army by using the Xiangjiang as a natural barrier.

In the critical battle that ensued, the commanders and fighters fought heroically against the enemy for seven days and nights at Quanxian County in Guangxi and suffered heavy casualties before they defeated the forces of the Kuomintang warlords by breaking through the fourth blockade line, the last line after leaving the Central Revolutionary Base Area, and forcing their way across the Xiangjiang. Thus the Red Army shook off 400,000 enemy troops and put an end to the enemy's scheme to destroy the Red Army. This victory testified once again: Before the iron and invincible will of the Red Army soldiers, all the enemy's plans of pursuits, encirclements, obstructions and interceptions were in vain.

2 *Crossing the Xiangjiang River*

After crossing the Xiangjiang, the Political Bureau of the Chinese Communist Party's Central Committee decided, at a meeting in Liping, Guizhou Province, to head straight for Guizhou where the enemy force was weak. In January 1935, the Red Army crossed the Wujiang River and captured the city of Zunyi.

At Zunyi the Central Committee of the Chinese Communist Party convened an enlarged meeting of the Political Bureau which ended the "Left" opportunist line led by Wang Ming and established Chairman Mao Zedong's leading position in the Red Army and the Central Committee. The decisions made here saved the Red Army and Central Committee at a critical moment and ensured the successful conclusion of the Long March to open a new way for the Chinese revolution. This was a turning-point of vital importance in the history of the Chinese Communist Party.

The decisions of the Zunyi Meeting filled the whole army with hope. It was as if the troops gained a new life with Chairman Mao as their leader. They became courageous as a dragon and lively as a tiger. On February 28, in the battle to recapture Zunyi, we won our first great victory since setting out on the Long March by destroying 20 regiments of the enemy troops and taking some 3,000 captives.

The captives, formerly labouring people who served in the Kuomintang army under force, were deeply affected by our rules for treating prisoners of war: "Do not kill or humiliate prisoners of war or search their pockets. Welcome those who are willing to join us and offer travel fees to those who want to go home." After a short period of education, most of the captives volunteered to join the Red Army.

This sketch shows captured officers and soldiers gathered before a meal.

3 *Great Victory at Zunyi*

After breaking through the fourth blockade line and crossing the Xiangjiang, the Red Army climbed over the noted high Laoshanjie Mountain in Yuechengling region and entered the area inhabited by the Miao people.

The Miaos, one of the minority nationalities in southwest China, are a brave and hard-working people. Most live in the Guizhou region and the rest in Yunnan or western Hunan. This sketch shows a Miao woman, whom we admired for being diligent, optimistic, strong and healthiy, carrying a basket on a shoulder hoe in a barefoot walk in the mountains.

The ancestors of the Miaos used to live in the fertile Changjiang River valley. But gradually reactionary rulers who plundered their land drove them to the poor remote mountains. The Miao people had to burn mountains to open up enough waste land to make a precarious living. In collusion with local despots, gentry and landlords, the man-eating officials forcibly annexed their land, forcing them to flee here and there. They never had a peaceful life. A Miao folk song goes like this: "No tree stems for crows to build their nests, no places for the Miaos to settle down. Driven about for many years, we never have a place of our own." Therefore, they heartily expressed support for the Chinese Communist Party and the Red Army who advocated equality for all nationalities.

4   A Miao Woman from Guizhou

It is an unforgettable scene.

It is ordinarily hot on sunny days in March in Yunnan Province. But a few days of intermittent drizzle had kept the weather cold by the time we came to a village on the Sichuan-Yunnan border.

It was still raining when we entered the home of a destitute family. What we saw frightened us. The family had four members: A middle-aged woman dressed in rags which could hardly cover the lower half of her body. A girl of 15-16 stood behind her father, without a piece of cloth covering her body. Weren't the nude women embarrassed in front of strangers? Yes, but too poor to have a meal a day, how could they afford clothes? The 65-year-old father in a worn-out shirt sat on a dog skin laid out on the ground by the fire. Heaving a sigh, he told us his sufferings with tears in his eyes. Many of us comforted him and offered some silk and cloth. He declined at first. Only after much persuasion from us, did he accept our gifts.

5　A Poor People's Home on the Sichuan-Yunnan Border

Oppressed and exploited by the Kuomintang warlords and local landlords, the poverty-stricken salt carriers in Guizhou and Sichuan lived worse than beasts of burden. They were in such extreme poverty that people in other regions could not imagine it. An old saying of the region —No three good days in a row, no flat land of three *li* and no salt carrier with three cents worth of silver — realistically reflected their hard life. Even in winter, peasants still wore patched thin cotton clothes. Conditions were worse for children who were stark naked in deep winter. As the Red Army passed by, we saw children standing on the roadside trembling with cold.

Since the poverty-stricken people could not find any other jobs, the young and strong had to carry salt throughout the year. It was a heavy work to cover a long distance with a basketful salt weighing 50-100 kilogrammes on the back. Over the years, they became hunchbacked and ached all over, but they never had enough food to eat.

These labouring people in the lowest stratum of society warmly welcomed the Red Army. Wherever we went, we found ourselves surrounded by the poor people from the vicinity. Streets of all the township we had visited were decorated with red flags and plastered with slogans to welcome us. Groups of people stood in the streets, reading leaflets, listening to speeches or staring at us with curiosity. We went into the masses to propagate our stand on going to the north to resist the Japanese invaders. Like kith and kin, we often had heart-to-heart talks with the local people. They told us about the exorbitant taxes and levies they were suffering and how cruelly the landlords had treated them. Every day a number of young people came to join us.

貴州·四川的千人爭（背塩的）

6 Salt Carriers in Guizhou and Sichuan

After crossing the Jinsha River, the Red Army continued northward to enter the Yi region. There had been a deep hatred between the Yis and the Hans. But the Red Army earnestly implemented its policies towards nationalities by establishing an alliance with the chieftain of the Guoji Tribe; advising the Laowu Tribe chieftain to remain neutral; and explaining our policies again and again to the chieftain of the Luohong Tribe who had been deceived by the Kuomintang agents and kept launching attacks on us. At last we convinced him that one of our consistent policies is to help minority nationalities attain complete liberation. Our policies were well-received by the Yi people. When we marched on, we often saw dishevelled and barefoot Yi people with hemp rugs over their shoulders jump down from mountain slopes to welcome us. They held high spears and broadswords, shouting in Yi language: "Long live the Red Army!"

All the Yis, men and women, wore cloak-shaped *caerwa* of hemp or sheep wool edged with pendants which came over the knees. Most chieftains wore dark blue *caerwa*. They served as guides and helped the Red Army do propaganda work. When we were fighting the enemy, the Yis also came to our aid with spears and broadswords.

This is a sketch of a junior chieftain, named Erhualuo, who was glad to act as our guide. After we gave him a gun, he expressed his appreciation in return by presenting us his blue *caerwa*. But we declined.

这是又一个头叫二花罢，他很高兴的望我们引路。我们送了他一支枪，他真高兴极了。

Influenced by the Party's policies towards all nationalities, Xiao Yuedan, the chieftain of the Guoji Tribe, pledged according to the Yi custom a sworn brotherhood with General Liu Bocheng, Chief-of-Staff of the Red Army and Commander of the Advance Force.

One day when Liu Bocheng met Xiao Yuedan at Qingshui Pond, the Yi chieftain made the suggestion that they become sworn brothers. Without hesitation, Liu agreed. Immediately, Xiao Yuedan had his assistant bring two bowls of clear water from a pond and a big rooster. A Yi man, holding the rooster with one hand, and a knife with the other, said: "On this day, in this month, the commander and Xiao Yuedan pledge to be sworn brothers. If a member breaks an oath, may he be killed like the rooster." So saying, he cut the rooster's head off and dropped its blood into the bowls. Xiao Yuedan let Liu Bocheng drink first. Taking the bowl, Liu repeated the oath and downed the liquid. "Good!" Xiao Yuedan burst into laughter, swore the oath and drank the other bowl.

Then Commander Liu presented Xiao Yuedan a red flag embroidered with the characters: "Guoji Tribe Guerrilla Detachment of the Chinese Red Army." The news was soon widespread. Next day, when Xiao Yuedan's uncle led the Red Army into the Yi region, clusters of Yi people, instead of suspecting us, stood by the roadside with no attempt to guard against us or block us, and stared in curiosity at our highly disciplined troops which did not commit the slightest offence against the civilians. They believed that the alliance between the Red Army commander and their chieftain was genuine and the Red Army would not encroach on their interests. With the help of the Yi people and Xiao Yuedan, the Red Army passed the mysterious Yi region in a sincere and happy atmosphere, continuing their march towards Anshunchang.

8 Yi Guerrillas of the Red Army

Anshunchang was an important wharf on the Dadu River. May of 1863 saw the army, 100,000 strong, of the Taiping Heavenly Kingdom under Prince Yi, Shi Dakai, encircled and frustrated by the Qing troops. Shi Dakai himself was killed. When the Red Army approached Anshunchang, they also faced great difficulties. Before them on the opposite bank of the Dadu River, a natural barrier, was the wharf occupied by Sichuan warlord troops; behind them came the main forces of the Kuomintang; and in the southwest lay the sparsely populated minority nationality regions. Chiang Kai-shek was beyond himself with delight on hearing that the Red Army was heading for the Dadu River. He sent aeroplanes to distribute propaganda leaflets expressing his hope that the Red Army might meet with the same fate as that of Shi Dakai at the Dadu River.

But the Red Army led by the Communist Party was invincible, capable of overcoming all kinds of difficulties, be they steep mountains or turbulent rivers. Shi Dakai was defeated at Anshunchang, but the heroic Red Army successfully crossed the Dadu River, reached the northern bank, and crushed the opposition.

The first group who wrought this wonder was 17 fighters from the Second Company under the First Regiment of the Red Army. With 300 metres in width and more than a dozen metres in depth, the river had a swift current of four metres a second, high waves and numerous whirlpools. Headed by the Company Commander Xiong Shanglin, 17 valiant fighters jumped on a ferryboat, forged ahead under a hail of bullets and reached the opposite shore. Jumping on the bank, they launched a fierce attack on the enemy and put the wharf under their control. The great success of the First Regiment of the Red Army enabled troops on the left rear flank to occupy the Luding Bridge. Then thousands of Red Army soldiers crossed the Dadu River. Their achievement put an end to Chiang Kai-shek's dream of turning the Red Army into another Shi Dakai. And the heroic crossing of the Dadu River by the 17 valiant fighters will be told among the people throughout the ages.

9 *Anshunchang (name of a wharf)*

Luding Bridge over the Dadu River in Luding County is 100 metres long, 2.8 metres wide. Clearance between the bridge deck and the river surface in the low water season is 14.5 metres. The bridge consists of 13 iron chains — nine of which are parallel to support planks while the other four serve as railings — fixed at either bank. People walking across the middle are often scared out of their wits as the bridge sways badly from left to right above the roaring water .

Before the Red Army came, the enemy had destroyed all the planks, leaving only the chains. No other bridge and ferry could be found. On the opposite bank, two brigades of enemy troops were stationed near the bridge and the pavilion at its end as well as in the mountains. They concentrated fire at the bridge end on our side, shooting without stopping. They shouted in arrogance: "If you were able to fly over, we would lay down our arms."

But the Red Army soldiers replied in a strong voice: "We don't want your arms but your bridge."

After careful surveillance, we deployed our forces and gathered our planks. The Second Company of the Fourth Regiment selected 22 heroes to form an advance force headed by Liao Dazhu, the company commander. Each brought with him a pistol, hand-grenades and sabre. The rest, holding rifles, followed closely while the Third Company comrades lay planks for the rear troops.

As soon as the bugle call to charge sounded, cannons and guns started to roar, shaking the surrounding valleys. The 22 heroes grasped the iron railings and moved ahead under a hail of bullets. As they were nearing the other end the enemy set fire to the pavilion in an attempt to stop them. The Red Army soldiers, however, continued their charge despite raging flames which scorched their clothes, caps, brows and hair. They rushed into the streets to fight the enemy. With the help of the follow-up units, they crushed the enemy and captured the Luding Bridge after a fierce fighting.

10 Luding Bridge

Marching in the remote and sparsely-populated mountain areas, the Red Army — rather than spending nights under a roof — often ate exposed to the wind and slept on the dump earth. In the virgin forests on the Xikang-Tibet Plateau, we often put up during the night in the open air sleeping on the ground wrapped in blankets or simply sitting on the ground with guns in our arms. Due to fatigue, we could fall asleep in such conditions. But more often than not, the piercing cold woke us up by midnight. Though we hunched down and wrapped our blankets tightly around us, it was too cold to continue sleeping. The twinkling stars above us were just like diamonds scattered on a velvet curtain. Meanwhile, the giant peaks on all four sides made the valley seem like the bottom of a well. Here and there, sleepless soldiers lay awake talking in low voices. Everything was so silent that all sounds, distant or close, loud or soft, caught our ears: The sounds seemed to be now silkworms eating mulberry, then horses galloping in the pasture. Sometimes it seemed as if the spring water were sobbing and the waves were roaring. Without realizing it, we fell asleep again.

老林之夜

11 *A Night at Paotonggang*

After crossing the Dadu, we came to the Western Sichuan Plateau which presented before us a view of criss-crossing valleys and the rolling snow and ice peaks of the Jiajin Mountains — the first snow mountains on the Long March. The terrain here is high and steep, averaging 3,000 metres above sea level. The weather is frigid. Mountains over 4,500 metres above sea level are covered with snow all year round. The First Front Army overcame incredible difficulties in scaling the Jiajin before capturing Dawei and Maogong in northwestern Sichuan and successfully joining forces with the Fourth Front Army.

At the southern end of Mount Qionglai in northwest Baoxing, the Jiajin Mountains rose more than 4,000 metres above sea level. Looking at them from a distance, we saw snow peaks pierce the clouds. When we reached the foot of the mountains, the temperature suddenly dropped. The paths were hard and slippery. As we climbed, we became surrounded by snow with ice cliffs above and snow valleys below. The brightness was blinding. Digging footholds in the ice, comrades of the advanced squad moved one after another slowly but steadily. Sometimes they marched hand in hand.

As we went up higher and the paths became narrower and the mountains steeper, the going grew more difficult. A careless step would end your climb by sending you to the depths of the surrounding gorges. Meanwhile, the cold wind kicked up the snow which swirled around us. In the clouds and fog, the Red Army soldiers marched on in thin clothes which offered no protection against a cold snowstorm. The wind, as sharp as a knife, cut our faces. The air grew thinner and many of us scarcely able to breathe, began to feel dizzy and weak. Our legs trembled. For every step we took, we stooped and panted. Many weak and ill comrades died on the way.

High as the snow mountains are, still higher is the iron will of this iron Red Army! The flame of revolutionary enthusiasm melted the freezing cold in the Jiajin. Revolutionary friendship turned into invincible strength. Supporting each other, Red Army soldiers continued climbing until they reached the summit.

12 *Climbing the Jiajin Mountains*

As we approached the summit, a sharp wind blew up suddenly, viciously swirling the snow around us. Soon hailstones, as big as eggs, whistled down on us. The weather was changeable in the snow mountains: now the sun shone brightly, now it snowed. Sometimes it stormed or hailed. Hailstones were often so big that they could actually kill people. The local Tibetan people, unable to explain these changes, attributed them to the magic power of gods and ghosts for whom they erected temples and flagpoles in the mountains. No wonder the local guide warned us against speaking, laughing or sitting while we were climbing. Otherwise, he warned us, the god of the mountains would kill us. Though what he said was superstitious, it did manage to convey the real dangers of climbing in the snow mountains.

Despite howling wind and heavy snowstorms, all our fighters gathered strength for the final ascent. Soon we reached the top and had a good view of a snow world. After only a little rest, we excitedly started down. The snowstorm soon dropped, and it started drizzling. Now and then, we looked back on the vast expanse of snow mountains now left far behind. In spite of fatigue and cold weather, everyone of us smiled, and we could not refrain from singing: "Look, Comrades! The war has begun. Fix the bayonets and charge ahead!" Our songs shook the mountains.

下雪山的之児[?]

13 *Conquering the Snow Mountains*

After climbing over the Jiajin Mountains, we came to a serf's home in a Tibetan community where peasants lived in stone houses and herdsmen in tents. The south-facing houses had a strong national flavour with flat roofs, many windows, simple style and plain colour. Generally the walls were constructed from stones or rammed-earth. The rooms upstairs were for living while those downstairs were for warehouses and livestock sheds. The houses were usually surrounded by courtyards.

This sketch shows a simple and crude building surrounded by a bamboo fence. It has two stories, the family housed on the second floor and oxen on the ground. The ladder is only a single log with a number of steps dug on it. Behind the house is a high narrow paper flag which stands as an offering to gods. Inside the house, almost no furniture can be seen.

Why were the Tibetan people so poverty-stricken? The feudal ruling system of integrating religion with politics was carried out in the Tibetan communities. The local government in the hands of feudal lama lords, was established on a reactionary, dark, cruel and savage serf system. Tibet was rigidly stratified: Officials, aristocracy, lords and their agents accounted for five per cent of the total population and serfs more than 90 per cent who had neither land nor freedom of person. The remaining five per cent were slaves who had no means of production or freedom. They suffered the cruelest exploitation and oppression while doing all kinds of heavy work all their lives.

Serfs had to pay rent in kind and in money besides performing corvée. Under a system of more than 100 kinds of taxes, a serf would pay numerous kinds of taxes in his life time. Many families, exploited by usurious loans, broke up or became beggars or slaves.

14 *In a Tibetan Village*

As we often cooked our meals by ourselves on the Long March, we all knew much about pots. The sketch shows three kinds of pots we used during that time: The first is used by the Tibetan people in Sichuan, the second by the Miaos in Guizhou and the third is the most popular.

The kinds of food cooked in the pots also describes the Red Army's hard life on the Qinghai-Tibet Plateau where we had difficulty breathing in the thin air of the high terrain. The water was often boiling before the temperature reached 100 degrees centigrade. Now there was *qingke* barley in our pots, now grassroots and edible wild herbs. Sometimes we made steamed bread mixing barley with wild herbs. But occasionally, we had nothing in pots.

In the vast wild grasslands, we were often in extreme difficulty. When night fell, we sought a place to set up camp. After that we gathered firewood and dry grassroots, put *qingke* barley in our pots and cooked our meals. More often than not it rained hard. We had neither tents nor houses to get shelter. Some of us held old umbrellas over head while sitting on small packages with water flowing underfoot. Since it was impossible to cook food, we had to settle for powdered *qingke* barley to fill our stomach.

Some troops crossed the grassland three times. The last time, which took more than a dozen days, was the most difficult. The troops were short of grain. The commanders had to have their battle horses killed. Soldiers began to eat the yaks which carried the tents or stewed and baked their leather belts and hats. They also mixed grass with a handful of fried flour to make a pot of flour porridge. Since the advance troops had eaten up all the known edible grass, the rear army had to try plants which had never been eaten. Some died from eating poisonous grass. The higher leaders gave orders to be careful to choose grass with no smell or bitter taste and cook it before eating. But the stewed grass could only fill our stomachs rather than increase our strength.

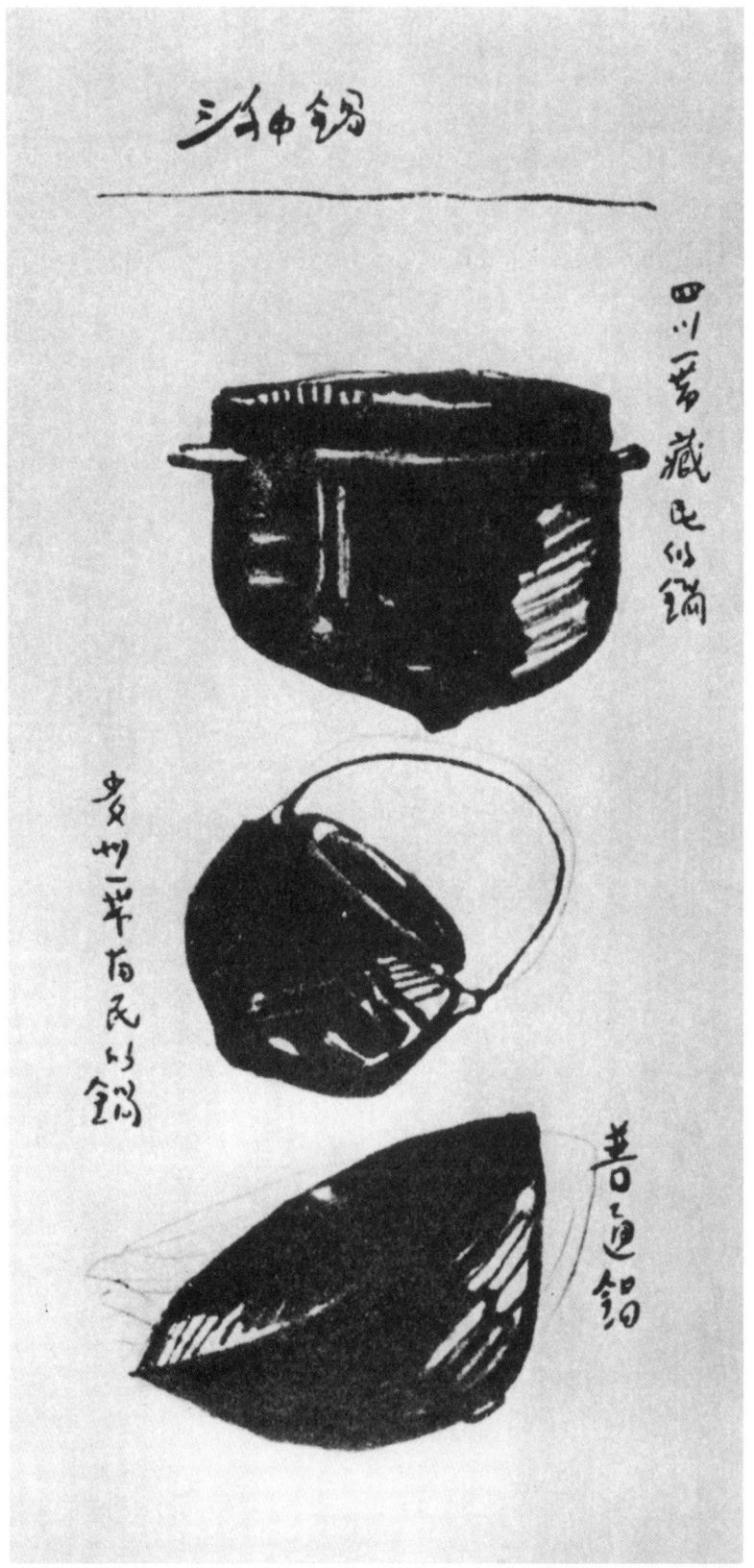

三种锅

四川草藏区的锅

贵州平苗民的锅

普通铝

15 *Three Kinds of Pots*

Tibetan communities are the homeland of yaks. Covered with long hair, the yak is a cold-resistant animal with a wide body. Living on the frigid Qinghai-Tibet Plateau, 3,000 metres above sea level, the animal can run fast and carry a heavy load. As we had never seen it before, it was a strange thing to us.

Domestic yaks, like the cow, are ruminant animals. There are also wild yaks. The yak, the main livestock of the Tibetan people, has a high economic value. The main means of transportation, it also supplies people with meat. Also called "boat on the highland," the yak is good at carrying supplies in the high and steep mountains. When the Red Army passed the Tibetan region, the yak played an important role in transportation. However, ferocious wild yaks live in different places during different times of the year. They gather in the plain by lakes in winter and come to the bitterly cold region to mate and breed between summer and autumn. A wild yak can provide 500 kilogrammes of meat. Fresh and delicious chunks of yak meat — eaten by hand — was a Tibetan herdsman's favourite food. The yak's yellow milk, rich in oil (more than six per cent) is suited to making butter. Its hair can be made into capes, tents and rope, and its skin provides good material for leather goods. Woollen sweaters woven with the yak's hair — which are sold on domestic and international markets — are beautiful, soft and warm. But it is not an easy job to capture a wild yak. Usually, people do not dare to offend it. Once offended, it might rush madly at you with the strength to overturn a truck.

16 A Yak

On arrival at the Tibetan region, smokers began to worry. They could hardly find shredded tobacco for water pipes, let alone cigarettes. Later someone found a kind of herb as a substitute. Smokers went everywhere to gather it and made grass tobacco themselves. It of course had a different taste.

17 Using Herbs as Tobacco

Tibetan communities are located among rolling snow ranges with high terrain and cold weather. The local variety of barley known as *qingke*, the main agricultural produce, has a short growing period and cold- and drought-resistant characteristics. The Tibetan people grind fried barley and peas into powder and then mix them with butter tea or barley wine to make small glutinous cakes which are their main food. They are fond of home-made butter tea and milk tea made by stirring butter and hot tea in a special wooden tube.

Before entering the vast grasslands, we were given orders to prepare enough grain for seven days. In sparsely-populated Maoergai, we had difficulty finding grain. For fear of dying of hunger, we had no alternative but to cut barley growing in the fields which had turned light yellow. In the meantime, we went everywhere to look for the Tibetans to pay them for the grain.

After having prepared the barley by frying it, we began to search for millstones but could not find enough in Maoergai. In the house where we were stationed, we found the upper half of a mill, which was of no use to us without the other half. Since our host had built his house with stones — thin slabs for the roof and thick ones for the walls — it was easy for me to get a stone. With the sabre of our team leader, I began to carve the lower half of the mill. Soon I finished my carving. Though our mill was small and irregular, we could grind more than 15 kilogrammes of barley in a day and night. It not only solved our problem, but also provided ground barley powder for other troops. The large square stone is shown in this sketch under the upper round millstone.

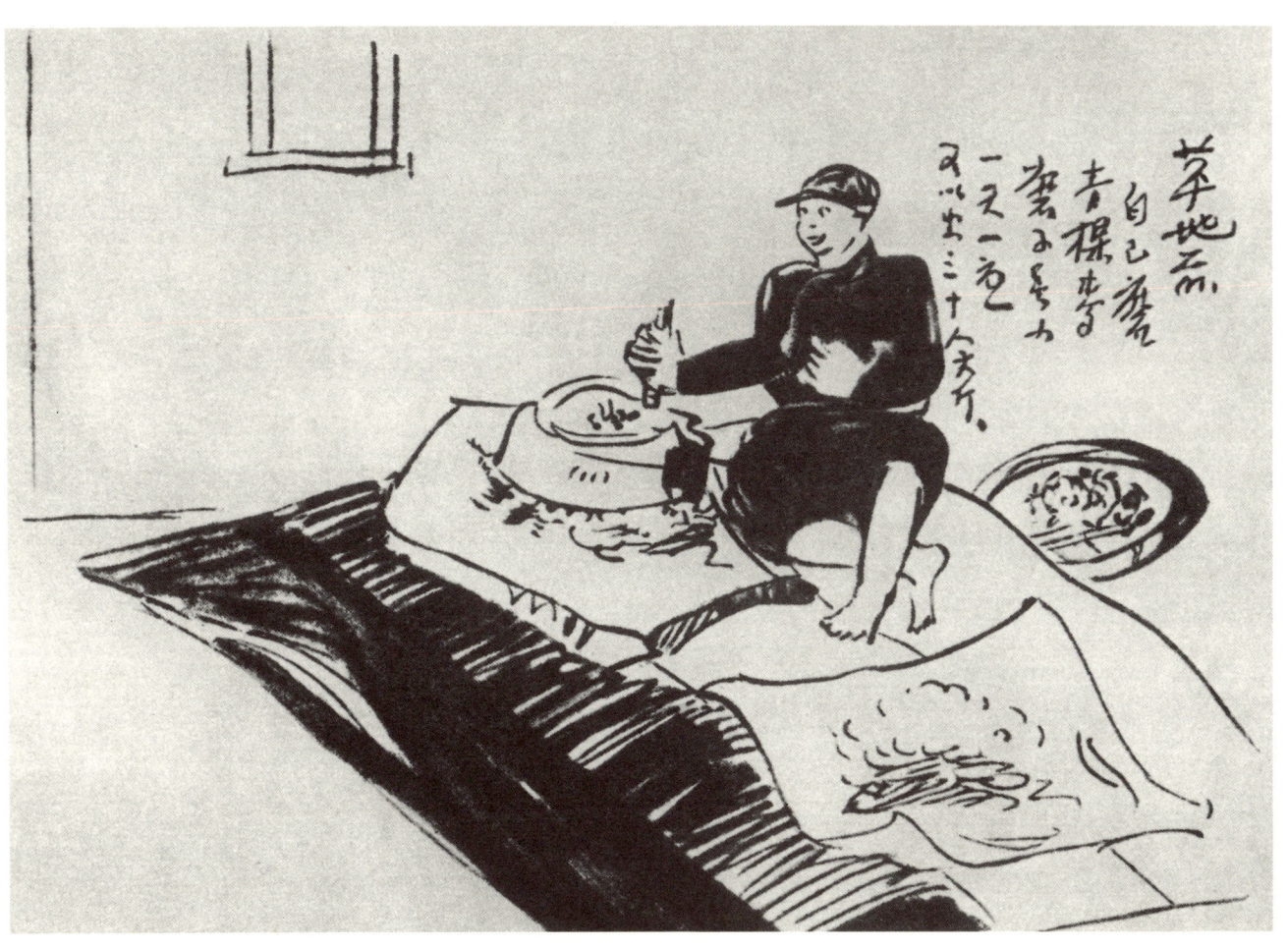

18 *Grinding Qingke Barley*

After a hard journey of seven days and nights, we finally came out of the vast grasslands and arrived at Banyou which lies at their edge. The last day, instead of raining, was a fine sunny day. Generally, people who have suffered from cold and hunger during a long hard trip are worn out. But the Red Army soldiers were still in high spirits, singing and laughing and going on their march with great strides.

In Banyou, you could see houses built with cow dung, herdsmen's shelters from the rain. We were going down towards the station in Panzhou Village below the grasslands. Though the grasslands are comparatively flat, they are also more than several thousand metres above sea level. We took up quarters inside houses, propped up pots and made pancakes with barley powder. This was the best food we had in the Tibetan region.

19 Making Pancakes

While marching in the grasslands, everyone of us had a grain sack on his back, which contained either fried or powdered barley. But we still suffered hunger. Before setting up camps, we could gather a few pieces of firewood and dry grassroots to boil some water. If we had had rice then, we could not have got enough firewood to cook it. Soaked in the rain, our barley powder had already congealed into glutinous lumps. But mixed with boiling water, it could be eaten to avoid hunger. Conditions were worse for those who had only barley which the rain had turned into a substance like rubber. One's teeth began aching from chewing the soaked barley long before one's stomach was full. Though we suffered hunger and fatigue in the night, we still had to cover 30 to 40 kilometres the following day.

If someone fell down, dropping his grain sack into poisonous water, he was faced with a hard dilemma: if he did not want to eat the barley, he went hungry. However, if he did, he risked suffering a bloated and aching stomach. Some people saw their grain spill into dirty mud after their sacks had gotten caught and torn on grassroots. They could do nothing but rely on other people's support.

20 *Carrying Grains Across the Grasslands*

Confronted with a vast stretch of desolate grasslands enveloped in a dark and dense fog, we were startled. We could hardly tell where we were going. Hidden ditches and rivers criss-crossed the wild grass, and dark stagnant water gave off a foul smell. Trudging through sodden quagmires covered with rotten grass and stems required great attention. If not careful, you could easily sink in so deep that it was difficult to pull your legs out. One by one, we followed our guide closely, picking our way carefully. Some mules and horses dropped into quagmires. They tried desperately to get out while sinking deeper and deeper until they disappeared in the marsh. People could do nothing to save them. The evil quagmires quickly resumed their original appearance.

The further we went into the grasslands the more difficulties we had. The weather was always dark and cloudy. More often than not, we were beset by rain and wind. Suddenly the world became small with only a tiny patch of sky above us. The sun disappeared and hid behind the clouds even after it had rained. We walked all day long but only covered a short distance before it got dark. There were no houses or even a single tree growing in the land. Most of us slept in the open air, only a few in camps.

The cold at night was almost unbearable. Even those who stayed in tents were stirred by the penetrating rain when there was a storm outside. We had to sit on the ground back to back under the shelter of bamboo hats or umbrellas. For those who did not have any tent, they soon got soaked, and the ground was covered with rain water. Standing in the rain, they looked forward to the coming of daybreak. Every time we continued our march after a cold and hungry night, we left some comrades lying forever on the ground where we had camped together the night before.

21 Camping in the Grasslands

This sketch shows a Red Army company marching in the grasslands.

Every company was faced with a stern test on crossing the snow mountains and grasslands. Though it was difficult to march in grasslands and we were threatened by hunger, cold, diseases and death, the Red Army soldiers forged ahead with energy, confident of winning the victory of revolution. The optimistic soldiers seemed not to know the meaning of hardship and worry. With revolutionary enthusiasm, they were able to overcome all kinds of hardships.

In high spirits, soldiers sang along the way with red flags fluttering in the wind. Shouldering heavy loads, the comrades of the mess squad had a harder journey. But they were the most energetic while their pots, knives and

22 *March in the Grasslands*

basins banged together with a clatter. Sometimes they whistled and ran fast as if they were not carrying 20 to 40 kilogrammes on their shoulders. At night, the grasslands were enveloped by dense fog. The troops picked high places to set up camps. If the weather was good, we got some firewood and lit bonfires and sang happily.

People grew weaker due to cold, hunger and bad weather along the hard trip. Some of us were too weak to walk. But we recalled Chairman Mao Zedong's words: We united more closely in difficult conditions. Stronger comrades supported the comrades in bad health. A team was organized to carry the wounded soldiers with the horses of commanders and other animals.

Comrade Dong Zhentang (1895-1937) was once a high-ranking officer in the Northwest Army founded by General Feng Yuxiang. In 1931, the 26th Route Army was given an order by Chiang Kai-shek to attack the Red Army in Jiangxi. Dong Zhentang, then a brigade commander, was discontented with Chiang Kai-shek's policies of civil war and non-resistance against the Japanese aggressors. Together with Zhao Bosheng, the chief-of-staff of the army, Ji Zhentong and Huang Zhongyue, he led the army of 17,000 to revolt and cross over to join the Red Army in Ningdu, Jiangxi Province on December 14, 1931. The insurgent troops were classified as the Fifth Army Corps of the First Front Army of the Chinese Workers' and Peasants' Red Army. Dong Zhentang was appointed commander of the Army Corps as well as commander of the 13th Army. When the Long March started, he was the commander of the Fifth Army Corps. After the successful conclusion of the Long March, he gave his life in a battle against the Kuomintang troops in Gaotai, Gansu Province on January 20, 1937.

The Fifth Army Corps undertook rear guard action during the Long March. Dong Zhentang led commanders and fighters in overcoming hardships and difficulties. They heroically resisted pursuing enemy troops more than ten times their number to protect the whole Red Army at the cost of heavy casualties. In January 1935, he took part in the Zunyi Meeting as commander of the Fifth Army Corps. Full of energy, he always looked simple and tidy in a grey uniform of home-made cloth and straw shoes. He was alert, calm, firm and brave during battle, a good example for army commanders. He always carried his pistol with him and had a habit of standing with one hand on his hip while holding a short pole in the other hand. He was kind towards his soldiers and showed concern for them. He often let the wounded ride his horse while he himself walked. Sometimes he carried rifles for his men, thus winning the deep love and respect of commanders and fighters.

董振堂同志

他手臂高举
欢喜又坚一根
短枪他是高
不了一支于
枪是囿一刻
钟都不会离
身的他那乘和
气!

23 Comrade Dong Zhentang

After breaking through Lazikou, a strategic pass, the Red Army began to scale Mount Minshan. In the end, we crossed the grasslands, came out of the Tibetan region and arrived at Hadapu between Minxian and Xigu counties in south Gansu Province, which is a region inhabited mostly by the Han and Hui people. The people there were overjoyed to see with their own eyes that the Red Army had given the warlords, who had cruelly oppressed them, a hard blow. Happily, they welcomed the Red Army as though we were their own family members.

At a meeting of commanders and cadres held by the Central Committee of the Chinese Communist Party, Chairman Mao pointed out that after the Long March of over 10,000 kilometres, our experienced and heroic commanders who had prevailed in so many battles through prudent and flexible tactics would be bound to attain the goal of going north to resist Japan.

"If we fail to reach the Great Wall, we are not men!" Chairman Mao Zedong's words pointed out a distinct direction for the Red Army and gave us boundless strength. Full of confidence, the Red Army eventually broke through the enemy's cordons, scaled Mount Liupan and entered the base areas on the Shaanxi-Gansu border.

In October 1935, the Red Army joined forces with the Northwest Red Army at Wuqi Township in Northern Shaanxi after covering a distance of 12,500 kilometres and fighting its way through 11 provinces. Then in October 1936, with the meeting at Huining, Gansu Province of the three main forces of the Red Army — the First, Second and Fourth Front armies — the Long March was triumphantly brought to an end. From that time on, the Red Army guided by the Chinese Communist Party strived to implement the policy of establishing an Anti-Japanese National United Front and prepared for the upsurge of resistance against Japan.

24 Arriving at Hadapu in Minxian County

History of the Long March Sketches

Sketches on the Long March was first printed in 1938 as *Sketches on the Journey to the West* at a time when our country was suffering the cruelest aggression by Japanese imperialism. The Kuomintang had fled all the way to Chongqing. The Eighth Route Army and the New Fourth Army were engaged in struggle deep in the rear areas of the enemy, thrusting into its heart. People in the Japanese occupied and rear areas controlled by the enemy were especially in need of great moral inspiration. It was in those days that I was overjoyed to have obtained the photo reproduction of *Sketches on the Long March*.

Thanks to the assistance of some enthusiastic friends, we had set up in Shanghai a publishing institution called "Wind and Rain Publishing House" where we published a monthly *Documents* supporting the War of Resistance Against Japanese Aggression. Because *Documents* carried speeches and articles by Chairman Mao Zedong and other leaders of our Party and also news and photos of the Eighth Route Army and the New Fourth Army, it was constantly subjected to the threat of imperialism and the so-called underground organizations of the Kuomintang. And later, even friends — under the threat of the Kuomintang — advised us time and again to be more "prudent". The danger of being banned and arrested was always at hand. Under these circumstances, we were uncertain whether an attempt to publish *Sketches on the Long March* in *Documents* could be completed and whether the photos of the sketches might not get damaged or lost. However, considering its impact, we felt it all the more imperative to race against time to edit and print it as swiftly and completely as possible.

This was how the first edition of *Sketches on the Long March* came to be published in 1938. It was first entitled *Sketches on the Journey to the West* because the Chinese translation of the book *Red Star over China* by American journalist Edgar Snow about his visit to Yan'an had just been published under the Chinese title *Notes on the Journey to the West*. A special chapter in the book was about the Long March, and since conditions at that time did not permit the use of the term "25,000-*li* Long March," we came up with a title we hoped readers might easily associate with the Long March. We chose the sketch of Comrade Lin Boqu as the first one in the book and also printed at its beginning a chronicle and a map of the Long March. I also wrote an introduction to it. Excerpts of which are as follows:

"... Although only 24 in number, these sketches have fully captured the greatness and firmness of the Chinese people in an art form which, like the nation, evolved from suffering and struggle.

"In Chinese paintings, who has ever described such a great theme, and who has ever depicted such persistent struggle? What a will that shakes heaven and earth, moves monsters and gods — hard working and diligent, being able to endure hardships, willing to stand anything with pleasure for the liberation of their nation. And now for the first time this will has found expression in these realistic and optimistic paintings....

"Then, after a long journey, these paintings and drawings were brought from the remote northern Shaanxi to the south. They will be always remembered along with the great historic event of the 25,000-*li* Long March. And their publication will also give a new great impetus to and mark the beginning of new development of Chinese art.

"The war against aggression which has given expression to the great will of this nation is now unfolding continuously. The broad masses of the Chinese people are selflessly enduring untold sufferings for their national survival. This is a further display of the national spirit expressed in these paintings. The publication of these paintings will also provide all just-minded people the world over with yet more historic proof that China's War of Resistance Against Japanese Aggression is bound to triumph.... "

These passages were written in a roundabout way and were not as explicit and penetrating as they could have been. Words like "class" were left out. The revolutionary optimism expressed by the sketches was not emphasized, nor were the relations between art and life elaborated. Still less did we realize that these were the initial manifestations of Chairman Mao's Thought in the field of literature and art. However, they truly reflected our firm belief in the victory of the revolution and the victory of the anti-Japanese war, and also our irrepressible and fervent emotions at the time. We edited quickly and printed a fine edition of 2,000 copies in photogravure and glossy papers, most of which were circulated in Shanghai and those areas under the control of the New Fourth Army. As a result, they greatly raised the morale of the fighters and people. Not long afterwards, as we had expected, the "Wind and Rain Publishing House" was ransacked and people working there were arrested.

Twenty years elapsed. In 1958, an enthusiastic reader discovered the book by chance at the Beijing Library. He considered this to be a very important historical record. Indeed, till this day, we have not found any other works of art actually produced during the Long March reflecting the life of the Long March and depicting the hardships and the revolutionary optimism of that time. So the People's Fine Arts Publishing House accepted the suggestion and reproduced in December of the same year 3,000 copies using mine as the master copy. After so many years of war, confiscation and prohibition, natural calamities and losses, there were indeed few copies left.

It was also at this time that the question of the identity of the artist first came up. At the time of the first printing, we only knew that the album had been sent to us by Comrade Xiao Hua. So we acknowledged him as the artist without making a check. At the time of its reprinting, when we asked him to write a preface, we came to know that he in fact was not the artist. But even Comrade Xiao Hua could not remember who the painter was. In his judgement, "the painter was most probably someone doing publicity work in the Fifth Army Corps." It was not until 1961 when Comrade Huang Zhen returned from abroad and Comrade Li Kenong mentioned this book to him that we finally found the artist. Huang Zhen was able to verify that these were actually painted by him during the Long March on papers of different kinds, sizes and colours which he could lay his hand on at that time. After 25 years, we were delighted to have found the artist whose spirit was just as optimistic and happy as that manifested in his paintings. Unfortunately the original paintings could not be located. This new edition is a reproduction of the past edition. We sincerely hope that the missing originals can also be found some day so that more splendour can be added to our historical documents.

In commemorating the 20th anniversary of the publication of "Talks at the Yan'an Forum on Literature and Art" by Chairman Mao and the 35th anniversary of the founding of the People's Liberation Army, the People's Fine Arts Publishing House decided to print once again a fine edition of this album and to use the title *Sketches on the Long March*. We all agreed that had they not been swiftly printed then in an album, they might not have survived. For this reason, I was asked to write a few words which I was happy to do. The past 20 years and more have witnessed vast changes. Comrade Li Yi and Comrade Chen Yiyu who worked together with me in editing and publishing the album have passed away. I wish to mention their names in memory.

In order to be true to the original, comrades from the People's Fine Arts Publishing House and the Beijing New China Printing House have overcome many difficulties in the process of printing, and have made it more attractive. This also shows the ardent love people cherish for this album about the Long March.

A Ying[1]

June 1962

---

[1] A Ying (1900-1977) was a contemporary writer and literary historian. He joined the Chinese Communist Party in 1926, and served as Director of the Bureau of Culture of Tianjin and Secretary-General of All-China Federation of Literary and Art Circles in post-liberation years. His works include short stories, prose and play scripts.

About the Author

Born into a peasant family in Tongcheng County, Anhui Province in 1909, Huang Zhen began to show an interest in art at an early age. In his youth, the author was also strongly affected by the progressive trend of the May 4th Movement. In 1925, he left his homeland to study at Shanghai High School of Fine Arts. Upon graduation, he started his career as an educator, teaching painting at a middle school. Soon afterwards, he joined the revolution, participating in the noted Ningdu Revolt of December 14, 1931. Following the uprising of the 26th Route Army under Kuomintang command, Huang Zhen joined the Chinese Workers' and Peasants' Red Army and later participated in the 25,000-*li* Long March.

The sketches made along the way of the Long March record this great unparalleled event in which the Red Army men displayed unyielding revolutionary spirit, fearing neither hardship nor death in their courageous advance. Touched by their spirit, Huang Zhen took up his pen and started his creation. But the hard conditions made it difficult even to find a complete piece of paper. He had to pick up any scraps he could find on the way for his sketches. What we see in this collection is only a fragment of his original work most of which was lost during the war years.

After the Long March, the author worked in the northern liberated areas for a long time. He took part in the War of Resistance Against Japanese Aggression as well as the War of Liberation and held many posts before becoming a general.

After the founding of the People's Republic of China, he ended his military career and started to work at the Ministry of Foreign Affairs. He was appointed ambassador to Hungary, Indonesia, and France and later was named Deputy Minister of Foreign Affairs. After the publication of Shanghai Sino-American Joint Communique, he went to the United States to serve as director of the Liaison Office of the People's Republic of China to the United States. He returned in 1977 to become Minister of Culture. In 1981, he served as Chairman of the Commission for Cultural Relations with Foreign Countries.Huang died in 1989.

图书在版编目（CIP）数据

长征画集 / 黄镇　绘. —北京：外文出版社，2006
ISBN 7-119-04514-8
I. 长… II. 黄… III. 素描 - 作品集 - 中国 - 现代 IV.J224
中国版本图书馆 CIP 数据核字（2006）第 076854 号

责任编辑：李　芳
英文责编：贺　军
封面设计：蔡　荣
印刷监制：韩少乙

《长征画集》

黄　镇　绘著

*

©外文出版社

外文出版社出版
（中国北京百万庄大街 24 号）
邮政编码 100037
外文出版社网址：http://www.flp.com.cn
外文出版社电子信箱：info@flp.com.cn sales@flp.com.cn
北京京都六环印刷厂印刷
中国国际图书贸易总公司发行
（中国北京车公庄西路 35 号）
北京邮政信箱第 399 号　邮政编码 100044
2006 年(16 开)第 1 版
2006 年第 1 版第 1 次印刷
（英）
ISBN 7-119-04514-8
06800　（精）
84-E-572S